FIRST GRADE READER

INSPIRING SHORT STORIES TEACHING LIFE SKILLS FOR KIDS AGES 6-8

A READING COMPREHENSION 1ST GRADE WORKBOOK

DR. FANATOMY
★★★★

NAME : ....

copyright@ dr. fanatomy 2025

All rights reserved. No part of this publication may be reproduced, distributed, or transmitted in any form or by any means, including photocopying, recording, or other electronic or mechanical methods, without the prior written permission of the publisher, except in the case of brief quotations embodied in critical reviews and certain other noncommercial uses permitted by copyright law.

This book is a work of non-fiction, and any resemblance to actual persons, living or dead, or actual events is purely coincidental.

The information and techniques described in this book are intended for educational and informational purposes only. The author and publisher shall not be held liable for any injury, damage, or loss arising from using or misusing the information presented in this book.

While every effort has been made to ensure the accuracy of the information contained within this book, the author and publisher make no warranties or representations express or implied, about the completeness, accuracy, reliability, suitability, or availability with respect to the contents of this book for any purpose. The use of any information provided in this book is at the reader's own risk.

TABLE OF CONTENTS

INTRODUCTION: WELCOME TO THE WONDERFUL WORLD OF STORIES! (Pg:4-8)

Purpose of the Book
- Let's embark on a magical journey filled with exciting stories that teach valuable life lessons!
- Develop strong reading comprehension skills while having fun.

How to Use This Book
- Step 1: Read the stories together. Take time to discuss the pictures and enjoy the journey.
- Step 2: Complete the reading comprehension activities after each story.
- Step 3: Talk about the life lessons and how they relate to your child's real life.

Tips for Parents
- Create a cozy and engaging reading environment.
- Ask open-ended questions about the story to encourage deeper understanding.
- Celebrate your child's progress and achievements to build their confidence.

Reading Comprehension Activities
Solution

CHAPTER 1: THE KINDNESS CORNER (Pg:9-16)

- **Story:** "The Little Bird Who Shared" (A bird shares its food with others.)
- **Life Lesson:** Sharing and helping others makes everyone happy.
- **Reading Comprehension Activities**
- **Solution**

CHAPTER 2 : HONESTY HEROES (Pg:17-25)

- **Story:** "Lila and the Lost Marble" (A child learns the importance of telling the truth.)
- **Life Lesson:** Honesty builds trust and makes us feel good about ourselves.
- **Reading Comprehension Activities**
- **Solution**

CHAPTER 3: TEAMWORK TRIUMPHS (Pg: 26-32)

- **Story:** "The Ants and the Gigantic Apple" (Ants work together to move a large apple.)
- **Life Lesson:** Teamwork helps us achieve amazing things.
- **Reading Comprehension Activities**
- **Solution**

CHAPTER 4: CONFIDENCE CHAMPIONS (Pg: 33-41)

- **Story:** "Max Tries Something New" (A child overcomes fear to try something new.)
- **Life Lesson:** Believing in yourself can lead to amazing discoveries
- **Reading Comprehension Activities**
- **Solution**

CHAPTER 5 : PATIENCE POWER (Pg: 42-49)

- **Story:** "The Caterpillar Who Waited" (A caterpillar patiently waits to become a butterfly.)
- **Life Lesson:** Good things take time and patience
- **Reading Comprehension Activities**
- **Solution**

CHAPTER 6: SHARING SPARKS JOY (Pg: 50-57)

- **Story:** "Mia and the Magic Crayons" (A child learns the joy of sharing her crayons.)
- **Life Lesson:** Sharing brings happiness to both the giver and the receiver.
- **Reading Comprehension Activities**
- **Solution**

CHAPTER 7: EARTH EXPLORERS (Pg: 58-65)

- **Story:** "Tommy and the Talking Tree" (A child learns the importance of protecting nature.)
- **Life Lesson:** Taking care of the planet is everyone's responsibility.
- **Reading Comprehension Activities**
- **Solution**

CHAPTER 8 : FEELING FANTASTIC (Pg: 66-74)

- **Story:** "Sasha's Cloudy Day" (A child learns to understand and express emotions.)
- **Life Lesson:** It's okay to have different feelings, and there are healthy ways to express them.
- **Reading Comprehension Activities**
- **Solution**

CHAPTER 9: FRIENDSHIP FLOWERS (Pg: 75-83)

- **Story:** "Charlie Finds a Friend" (A child learns the importance of friendship.)
- **Life Lesson:** Friends make life fun and meaningful.
- **Reading Comprehension Activities**
- **Solution**

CONCLUSION: YOU ARE A STAR! (Pg: 84-88)

APPENDIX TABLES (Pg: 89-92)

- Common Action Words (Verbs) for First Graders
- Emotion Words and How to Recognize Them
- Life Lessons from the Stories
- Easy Word Roots for Kids

Introduction: Welcome to the Wonderful World of Stories!

Welcome to the Wonderful World of Stories!

Stories have the incredible power to inspire, teach, and entertain. This book is your gateway to a magical journey where exciting tales capture your imagination and help you grow as a thoughtful reader.

Purpose of the Book

Embark on a Magical Journey:

- This book is more than just a collection of stories—it's a guide to exploring meaningful lessons hidden within every tale. Dive into adventures that will teach kindness, honesty, teamwork, and other life skills.

Develop Reading Comprehension Skills:

- Each story is paired with fun and thought-provoking activities designed to sharpen your understanding. From answering questions to exploring emotions, this book will make you a stronger and more confident reader.

How to Use This Book

Make the most of this reading adventure with these simple steps:

Step 1: Read the Stories Together
- Immerse yourself in the story by reading it aloud or taking turns reading with your child.
- Pause to discuss the colorful illustrations and imagine yourself in the characters' shoes.
- Take time to enjoy the journey, savoring every detail.

Step 2: Complete the Activities
- After each story, explore the reading comprehension activities.
- These activities include answering questions, solving puzzles, and imagining what could happen next.
- Each activity is designed to reinforce what you've learned from the story in a fun way.

Step 3: Reflect on the Life Lessons
- Talk about the moral of the story and how it relates to everyday life.
- Share personal experiences where these lessons apply.
- Use the stories as conversation starters to help your child think critically about the world around them.

Tips for Parents

As a parent, you play a key role in nurturing your child's love for stories and reading. Here are some ways to make this journey even more enriching:

Create a Cozy Reading Environment:
- Set up a special reading nook with soft pillows, a warm blanket, and good lighting.
- Let your child pick their favorite time of day to read together.

Ask Open-Ended Questions:
- Encourage deeper thinking by asking questions like, "Why do you think the character made that choice?" or "What would you have done in that situation?"
- Help your child connect the story to their own life or real-world events.

Celebrate Progress and Achievements:
- Praise your child for completing a story or mastering a new word.
- Use a sticker chart or other reward systems to recognize milestones in their reading journey.
- Highlight how much they've grown as a reader, reinforcing their confidence and excitement to keep learning.

What Awaits You in This Book

From tales of friendship and teamwork to lessons about honesty and patience, each chapter offers a unique opportunity to learn while having fun. You'll encounter:
- Stories featuring relatable characters facing challenges and triumphs.
- Activities to deepen comprehension and critical thinking skills.
- Life lessons that inspire kindness, perseverance, and empathy.

Let the Journey Begin!

As you turn the pages of this book, you're not just reading—you're building a lifelong love for stories and unlocking the joy of learning. So, gather your child, get cozy, and let's step into the wonderful world of stories together!

Chapter 1: The Kindness Corner

Welcome to the Kindness Corner!

This chapter features a delightful story and fun activities that will teach you the importance of sharing and helping others.

Story: "Sunny the Sharing Bird"

Sunny the bird loved to fly high in the sky! He would swoop and soar through the trees. One day, Sunny found a pile of yummy berries. "Yum! These are for me!" he chirped.

But then, Sunny saw two other birds. They looked sad and hungry. "I feel sorry for them," thought Sunny. So, he shared his berries with the other birds.

The other birds said, "Thank you, Sunny! You are so kind!" Sunny felt happy because he helped his friends.

A few days later, Sunny was flying when he bumped into a tree! "Ouch!" he cried. He couldn't fly very well.

The two birds Sunny helped saw him. They helped him back to his nest and brought him yummy worms to eat.

Sunny learned a big lesson: <u>**When you are kind to others, good things happen to you too!**</u>

QUESTION TIME

- Who found the berries?
- What did Sunny do with the berries?
- How did the other birds feel?
- What happened to Sunny later?
- Who helped Sunny?

EXPLORE THESE WORDS

- What does **"swoop"** mean in the sentence, "He would swoop and soar through the trees"?(Hint: Think about how a bird moves quickly through the air.)
- What does **"chirped"** mean when Sunny says, "Yum! These are for me!"? (Hint: How do birds usually make sounds?)
- What does **"sorry"** mean in the sentence, "I feel sorry for them"?(Hint: How do you feel when you see someone sad?)

EXPLORE THESE WORDS

- What does **"bumped"** mean in the sentence, "Sunny was flying when he bumped into a tree"? (Hint: What happens when you accidentally hit something?)
- What does **"lesson"** mean in the sentence, "Sunny learned a big lesson"? (Hint: What is something important that you learn?)

"SUNNY'S FEELINGS": MATCH THE FOLLOWING

Column A (Situation)	Column B (Emotion)
1. When Sunny finds the pile of berries	A. Sunny feels **happy and proud.**
2. When he sees the other birds are hungry	B. Sunny feels **sad and hurt.**
3. When he shares his berries	C. Sunny feels **excited**!
4. When he bumps into the tree	D. Sunny feels **grateful and happy.**
5. When the other birds help him	E. Sunny feels **sorry** for the other birds

ANSWERS

QUESTION TIME

- Who found the berries? (Sunny)
- What did Sunny do with the berries? (He shared them.)
- How did the other birds feel? (Happy)
- What happened to Sunny later? (He bumped into a tree.)
- Who helped Sunny? (The birds he helped)

EXPLORE THESE WORDS

- Swoop: To fly down quickly like a bird.
- Chirped: To make a short, happy sound like a bird.
- Sorry: Feeling sad for someone else.
- Bumped: To hit something by accident.
- Lesson: Something you learn.

"SUNNY'S FEELINGS": MATCH THE FOLLOWING

- 1 → C
- 2 → E
- 3 → A
- 4 → B
- 5 → D

Chapter 2 : Honesty Heroes

Story: The Honest Friend

Lila *loved playing marbles with her friends. One day, Jake brought a big, shiny marble to school. It was so pretty!*

When Lila held the marble, it slipped from her hand. It rolled across the playground and into a drain. Lila felt scared. Jake didn't see it happen.

That night, Lila felt very bad. Her tummy felt tight, and she couldn't sleep. She remembered what her mom always said: **"Telling the truth is always the right thing to do**."

The next day, Jake asked, "Has anyone seen my shiny marble?"

Lila took a deep breath and said, "Jake, I lost your marble. It rolled into the drain. I'm really sorry."

Jake looked sad but said, "Thanks for telling me. We're still friends!"

Mrs. Carter heard what happened. She smiled and said, "Lila, telling the truth was brave!" She gave Lila a gold sticker that said, "Honesty Hero."

Lila felt happy and proud. She learned that being honest is always the right thing to do!

Life Lesson:

Being honest makes people trust you and helps you feel proud of yourself.

QUESTION TIME

- What did Lila love playing with her friends?
- What did Jake bring to school?
- Where did the marble roll?
- How did Lila feel when she didn't tell Jake?
- What did Mrs. Carter give Lila?

MATCH THE FOLLOWING (FEELINGS AND ACTIONS)

Match Lila's feelings to what happened in the story:

What Happened	How Lila Felt
Lila dropped the marble.	A. Proud and happy
Lila didn't tell Jake about the marble.	B. Bad and upset inside
Lila told Jake the truth.	C. Relieved and glad
Jake said, "We're still friends!"	D. Excited and proud
Mrs. Carter gave Lila a gold sticker.	E. Nervous and scared

MATCH THE WORD TO ITS MEANING

Word	Meaning
Shiny	a) Not afraid to do something hard or scary.
Drain	b) Telling the truth and not lying.
Honest	c) Bright and reflecting light.
Brave	d) A pipe that carries away water.
Proud	e) Feeling happy about something you did well.

Please let us know how we're doing by leaving us a review.

ANSWERS

QUESTION TIME

- Marbles.
- A big, shiny marble.
- Into a drain.
- Her tummy felt funny.
- A gold sticker that said, "Honesty Hero."

MATCH THE FOLLOWING (FEELINGS AND ACTIONS)

- Lila dropped the marble. - E. Nervous and scared
- Lila didn't tell Jake about the marble. - B. Bad and upset inside
- Lila told Jake the truth. - C. Relieved and glad
- Jake said, "We're still friends!" - A. Proud and happy
- Mrs. Carter gave Lila a gold sticker. - D. Excited and proud

MATCH THE WORD TO ITS MEANING

1. Shiny - c) Bright and reflecting light.
2. Drain - d) A pipe that carries away water.
3. Honest - b) Telling the truth and not lying.
4. Brave - a) Not afraid to do something hard or scary.
5. Proud - e) Feeling happy about something you did well.

Chapter 3. Teamwork Triumphs

Story: The Ants and the Big Apple

One sunny day, a group of ants were walking together. Suddenly, they saw something amazing—a BIG, red apple! It was so big that even all the ants together couldn't lift it!

"Wow!" said Ant Max. "Let's take it home!"

But the apple was too heavy. "What can we do?" asked Ant Lily.

Ant Zoe had an idea. "Let's work as a team!"

All the ants lined up. Some pushed, some pulled, and some guided the apple. It was hard work! The apple rolled left and right, but the ants didn't stop.

Finally, they got the apple to their home. "We did it!" cheered Ant Max. "Teamwork is the best!"

The ants had a big feast and shared the apple. They learned that when they work together, they can do big things!

Life Lesson:
When we help each other, we can do amazing things!

MULTIPLE CHOICE QUESTIONS

Instructions: Circle the correct answer.

(1) What did the ants find?
- a) A banana
- b) An apple
- c) A rock

(2) Who said, "Let's work together"?
- a) Ant Max
- b) Ant Lily
- c) Ant Zoe

(3) What did the ants do to move the apple?
- a) They ate it.
- b) They pushed and pulled it.
- c) They left it.

(4) How did the ants feel at the end?
- a) Sad
- b) Happy
- c) Angry

TRUE OR FALSE

Instructions: Write T for True or F for False.

1. The ants found a small orange.
2. The apple was too big for one ant.
3. The ants worked alone.
4. The ants had a feast at the end.

FILL IN THE BLANKS

Instructions: Fill in the blanks with the correct words.

1. The ants found a big, red _____.
2. Ant _____ said, "Let's work together."
3. The ants _____ and _____ the apple.
4. The ants had a big _____ at the end.

ANSWERS

MULTIPLE CHOICE QUESTIONS

Answers:
1. b) An apple
2. c) Ant Zoe
3. b) They pushed and pulled it.
4. b) Happy

TRUE OR FALSE

Answers:
1. F
2. T
3. F
4. T

FILL IN THE BLANKS

1. apple
2. Zoe
3. pushed, pulled
4. feast

Please let us know how we're doing by leaving us a review.

Chapter 4: Confidence Champions

Story: Max Tries Something New

Max was a curious boy who loved watching the world around him. One sunny morning, Max saw a group of kids riding their bikes in the park.

They zoomed past him, laughing and waving. Max had a shiny red bike, but it had been sitting in the garage because he was too scared to try riding it.

"What if I fall?" Max thought nervously.

That evening, Max's mom noticed him sitting quietly by the window. She asked, "What's on your mind, Max?"

"I want to ride my bike, but I'm scared I might fall," he admitted.

Mom smiled and said, "Trying something new can be scary, but remember, every expert was once a beginner. Why don't we practice together?"

The next morning, Max and his mom went to the park with his shiny red bike. At first, Max felt shaky and wobbly.

He fell a few times, but Mom helped him get back up. "You're doing great, Max! Keep going," she encouraged.

After some practice, Max started to feel more balanced. Soon, he was riding his bike all by himself! "I'm doing it! I'm really doing it!" Max cheered, his face beaming with pride.

From that day on, Max couldn't stop riding his bike. He realized that trying something new wasn't as scary as he thought.

Life Lesson:

Believing in yourself can lead to amazing discoveries. Even if something feels scary at first, courage and practice can help you succeed.

MULTIPLE CHOICE QUESTIONS

1) What did Max feel at the beginning of the story?
   - a) Excited
   - b) Nervous or scared
   - c) Angry

2) What did Max's mom say to encourage him?
   - a) "You should give up."
   - b) "Every expert was once a beginner."
   - c) "Don't talk to me about it."

3) How did Max feel at the end of the story?
   - a) Sad
   - b) Happy and proud
   - c) Bored

4) What did Max learn about trying new things?
   - a) Trying new things is always easy.
   - b) Trying something new isn't as scary as it seems.
   - c) Trying new things is a waste of time.

DRAWING CONCLUSIONS

1. What did Max learn about trying new things?
2. Why was Max scared to ride his bike?
3. What did Max's mom do to help him?
4. Write one thing you were scared to try but ended up liking.
5. Draw a picture of something you want to try but feel a little scared about.

VOCABULARY MATCH

Match the word to its meaning:

Word	Meaning
1. Curious	a) Feeling happy about something you did.
2. Nervous	b) Being brave to try something hard.
3. Practice	c) Wanting to learn or know something.
4. Proud	d) Feeling scared or worried.
5. Courage	e) Doing something again to get better.

ANSWERS

MULTIPLE CHOICE QUESTIONS

Answers:
1. b) Nervous or scared
2. b) "Every expert was once a beginner."
3. b) Happy and proud
4. b) Trying something new isn't as scary as it seems.

DRAWING CONCLUSIONS

Answers:
1. Trying something new isn't as scary as it seems.
2. He was scared he might fall.
3. She practiced with him and encouraged him.
4. (Open-ended; example: "I was scared to swim, but now I love it!")

VOCABULARY MATCH

1. Curious – c) Wanting to learn or know something.
2. Nervous – d) Feeling scared or worried.
3. Practice – e) Doing something again to get better.
4. Proud – a) Feeling happy about something you did.
5. Courage – b) Being brave to try something hard.

5. Patience Power

Story: The Caterpillar Who Waited

Once upon a time, in a big, sunny garden filled with colorful flowers, there lived a little caterpillar named Coco. Coco loved to munch on green leaves and crawl around all day. But Coco had a BIG dream—he wanted to fly high in the sky like the beautiful butterflies he saw fluttering above him.

One sunny morning, Coco saw his friend Bella the Butterfly gracefully flying from flower to flower. "Bella, how can I fly like you?" Coco asked, his tiny eyes wide with curiosity.

Bella smiled and said, "You need to be patient, Coco. One day, you'll change into something amazing!"

Coco didn't quite understand, but he trusted Bella. He kept eating and growing until one day, he felt very, very sleepy.

He found a strong branch on a tall bush and spun a cozy little shell around himself called a chrysalis. Inside, he rested for many, many days.

This is taking forever!" Coco thought, feeling a little impatient. But he remembered Bella's words: Be patient. Good things take time.

Then, one magical morning, the chrysalis began to crack open. Coco stretched out his new, colorful wings and looked around in amazement. He had turned into a beautiful butterfly!

Coco flapped his wings and soared high into the sky. "I did it! Waiting was worth it!" he cheered.

From that day on, Coco always remembered: **Patience brings beautiful things.**

Life Lesson:

Just like Coco had to wait to become a butterfly, we also need to be patient in life. Whether it's waiting for our turn, watching a plant grow, or counting down to a special day, good things happen when we wait and work hard.

SEQUENCING THE BUTTERFLY'S LIFE CYCLE

Put the stages of Coco's life in the correct order by numbering them 1 to 4.

- Coco rests inside a chrysalis.
- Coco hatches from an egg as a tiny caterpillar.
- Coco turns into a butterfly and flies.
- Coco eats leaves and grows bigger.

UNDERSTANDING FIGURATIVE LANGUAGE – "TIME FLIES"

In the story, Coco waited for many days inside the chrysalis. People often say, "Time flies" when something feels like it happens quickly.

1. Does time really fly like a bird? (Yes / No)
2. What do you think "time flies" means?
3. Can you think of a time when you felt like time flew by?

MATCH THE FOLLOWING

Match the word on the left with its correct meaning on the right.

Word	Meaning
1. Patient	a) To change into something new.
2. Chrysalis	b) A cozy shell where a caterpillar rests.
3. Transform	c) Waiting calmly without complaining.
4. Dream	d) Something you hope for.
5. Butterfly	e) A beautiful insect with colorful wings.

FILL IN THE BLANK

Fill in the blanks with the correct word from the story:
Word Bank:
patient, chrysalis, transform, butterfly, happy
1. Coco wanted to fly like a _____.
2. Coco made a cozy _____ to rest in.
3. Bella told Coco to be _____ and wait.
4. Coco's dream was to _____ into a butterfly.
5. After waiting, Coco felt _____ and proud.

ANSWERS

SEQUENCING THE BUTTERFLY'S LIFE CYCLE

Answers:

1. Coco hatches from an egg as a tiny caterpillar.
2. Coco eats leaves and grows bigger.
3. Coco rests inside a chrysalis.
4. Coco turns into a butterfly and flies.

UNDERSTANDING FIGURATIVE LANGUAGE

Answers:
1. No.
2. It means time feels like it passes quickly.
3. (Open-ended; example: "When I was playing with my friends, time flew by!")

MATCH THE FOLLOWING

1. Patient – c) Waiting calmly without complaining.
2. Chrysalis – b) A cozy shell where a caterpillar rests.
3. Transform – a) To change into something new.
4. Dream – d) Something you hope for.
5. Butterfly – e) A beautiful insect with colorful wings.

FILL IN THE BLANK

Answers:

1. butterfly
2. chrysalis
3. patient
4. transform
5. happy

6. Sharing Sparks Joy

Story: Mia and the Magic Crayons

Mia loved to color. She had a big box of crayons with every color she could imagine—sunny yellow, ocean blue, and even sparkly silver! She carried them everywhere, always ready to draw something beautiful.

One day at school, Mia saw her friend Leo sitting quietly at his desk. "Why aren't you coloring, Leo?" Mia asked.

Leo sighed. "I forgot my crayons at home."

Mia looked at her big box of crayons. She had so many! She thought for a moment and then smiled. "You can use mine!" she said, handing him a few colors.

Leo's face lit up. "Really? Thank you, Mia!"

Soon, their friends Emma and Jake joined in, and Mia shared her crayons with them too. They all started drawing together—a bright yellow sun, a colorful rainbow, and a big green tree. Mia noticed something special—sharing her crayons made her heart feel warm and happy.

When she got home, Mia told her mom, "Today, I shared my crayons, and it felt like magic!"

Her mom hugged her and said, "That's because sharing brings joy—to you and to others."

Mia smiled, knowing she would always share her crayons and her happiness.

Life Lesson:

Sharing brings happiness! Just like Mia, we can feel happy when we share. Sharing helps us make friends and brings smiles to others. Whether it's sharing crayons, toys, or even kind words, giving to others makes the world a happier place!

POINT OF VIEW – MIA'S FEELINGS

How did Mia feel when she saw Leo without crayons?
1. a) Happy
2. b) Sad
3. c) Excited

How did Mia feel after she shared her crayons?
1. a) Angry
2. b) Happy and warm
3. c) Bored

MAKING INFERENCES – WHY SHARING FEELS GOOD

Why did Mia feel happy after sharing her crayons?
1. a) Because she got new crayons.
2. b) Because sharing made her and her friends happy.
3. c) Because she didn't like her crayons.

Have you ever shared something with a friend? How did it make you feel?

MATCH THE FOLLOWING

Match the word on the left with its correct meaning on the right.

Word	Meaning
Share	a) To give something to others.
Crayons	b) Tools used for drawing and coloring.
Joy	c) A feeling of happiness.
Friends	d) People you like and spend time with.
Magic	e) Something that feels special or amazing.

SEQUENCING THE STORY

ut the events of the story in the correct order by numbering them 1 to 5.

- Mia shares her crayons with Leo, Emma, and Jake.
- Mia sees Leo sitting quietly without crayons.
- Mia tells her mom how happy sharing made her feel.
- Mia and her friends draw a sun, a rainbow, and a tree together.
- Mia brings her big box of crayons to school.

ANSWERS

POINT OF VIEW – MIA'S FEELINGS

Answer Key:
1. b) Sad
2. b) Happy and warm

MAKING INFERENCES – WHY SHARING FEELS GOOD

Answer Key:
1. b) Because sharing made her and her friends happy.

FILL IN THE BLANK

Answers:

1. butterfly
2. chrysalis
3. patient
4. transform
5. happy

SEQUENCING THE STORY

1. Mia brings her big box of crayons to school.
2. Mia sees Leo sitting quietly without crayons.
3. Mia shares her crayons with Leo, Emma, and Jake.
4. Mia and her friends draw a sun, a rainbow, and a tree together.
5. Mia tells her mom how happy sharing made her feel.

7. Earth Explorers

Story: Tommy and the Talking Tree

Tommy loved playing in the park near his house. One sunny afternoon, he sat under a big, old tree to rest. Suddenly, he heard a soft voice.

"Tommy, can you hear me?"

Tommy looked around. No one was there. "Who's talking?" he asked.

"It's me—the tree!" said the voice.

Tommy's eyes widened. "Trees can talk?"

"Only to those who care," said the tree. "I need your help. People are cutting down trees, and animals are losing their homes."

Tommy thought for a moment. "That's not fair! Trees give us shade, clean air, and homes for birds and squirrels."

"Yes," said the tree. "If more children like you take care of nature, the world will be a better place."

From that day on, Tommy promised to protect trees. He told his friends never to litter, to plant more trees, and to care for nature.

And the tree, happy and safe, whispered a gentle "Thank you" in the wind.

Life Lesson:

Taking care of the planet is everyone's responsibility!

- Trees give us fresh air to breathe.
- Animals need trees for homes.
- We should never harm nature!

FACTS AND OPINIONS

Facts are things that are true. Opinions are what someone thinks or feels.

Read these sentences. Are they facts or opinions?
1. Trees give us oxygen.
2. Trees are the most beautiful part of nature.
3. Birds build nests in trees.
4. Everyone should love trees.

VOCABULARY MATCH

Match the word on the left with its correct meaning on the right.

Word	Meaning
1. Nature	a) To keep something safe.
2. Protect	b) Trash left on the ground.
3. Oxygen	c) The world around us, like trees and animals.
4. Litter	d) To speak very softly.
5. Whisper	e) The clean air we breathe.

FILL IN THE BLANKS

Fill in the blanks with the correct word from the story:
Word Bank:
park, homes, birds, protect, thank you

1. Tommy loved playing in the _____.
2. The tree told Tommy that animals are losing their _____.
3. Trees give us shade, clean air, and homes for _____ and squirrels.
4. Tommy promised to _____ trees and care for nature.
5. The tree whispered a gentle "_____" in the wind.

ANSWER THE FOLLOWING (ONE-WORD ANSWERS)

Answer the following questions in one word:

1. What did Tommy hear while sitting under the tree?
2. Who was talking to Tommy?
3. What do trees give us to breathe?
4. What did Tommy promise to do for nature?
5. How did the tree say "thank you" to Tommy?

ANSWERS

FACTS AND OPINIONS

1. Fact
2. Opinion
3. Fact
4. Opinion

VOCABULARY MATCH

1. Nature – c) The world around us, like trees and animals.
2. Protect – a) To keep something safe.
3. Oxygen – e) The clean air we breathe.
4. Litter – b) Trash left on the ground.
5. Whisper – d) To speak very softly.

FILL IN THE BLANKS

Answer Key:
1. park
2. homes
3. birds
4. protect
5. thank you

ANSWER THE FOLLOWING (ONE-WORD ANSWERS)

Answer Key:
1. Voice
2. Tree
3. Oxygen
4. Protect
5. Whisper

8. Feeling Fantastic

Story: Sasha's Cloudy Day

Sasha woke up feeling grumpy. The sky outside was gray, and rain tapped on her window.

"Ugh," she sighed. "A cloudy day."

At breakfast, things got worse. Her toast fell on the floor, and her milk spilled all over the table.

"This is the worst day ever!" Sasha said, feeling upset.

Her mom gave her a hug. "It's okay to feel sad sometimes, Sasha. Even on cloudy days, we can find ways to feel better. Let's build a fort!"

Sasha's frown turned into a small smile. She and her mom made a cozy fort with blankets, pillows, and chairs. They read stories, made shadow puppets, and laughed together.

Soon, Sasha felt warm and happy inside the fort. When she peeked outside, the sun was shining through the clouds.

"Mom," Sasha said, "I still wish it wasn't cloudy this morning, but I had a really fun day anyway!" Her mom smiled.

"See? Even when we feel down, we can find ways to feel better. It's okay to have all kinds of feelings, Sasha."

Life Lesson:

It's okay to feel happy, sad, or grumpy—just like the weather changes! When you feel down, you can talk to someone, do something fun, or find a new way to enjoy the day.

IDENTIFYING EMOTIONS

1) How did Sasha feel when she woke up?
a) Happy
b) Grumpy
c) Excited

2) How did Sasha feel when her toast fell and her milk spilled?
a) Frustrated
b) Calm
c) Sleepy

3) How did Sasha feel inside the fort?
a) Happy
b) Sad
c) Angry

COMPARING FEELINGS

1) How did Sasha's feelings change from the beginning to the end?
a) She stayed grumpy.
b) She felt happy and warm.
c) She felt sleepy.

2) What helped Sasha feel better?
a) Building a fort and playing with her mom.
b) Watching TV.
c) Eating more toast.

VOCABULARY MATCH

Match the word on the left with its correct meaning on the right.

Word	Meaning
1. Grumpy	a) Warm and comfortable.
2. Cozy	b) Bright light from the sun.
3. Fort	c) Feeling upset or annoyed.
4. Sunshine	d) A fun hiding place made with blankets.
5. Feelings	e) Emotions like happy, sad, or excited.

FILL IN THE BLANKS

Fill in the blanks with the correct word from the story:

Word Bank:
feelings, fort, warm, sunshine, grumpy

1. Sasha woke up feeling _____.
2. Sasha and her mom built a _____.
3. Inside the fort, Sasha felt _____ and happy.
4. The _____ started to shine through the clouds.
5. It's okay to have all kinds of _____.

Please let us know how we're doing by leaving us a review.

ANSWERS

IDENTIFYING EMOTIONS

Answer Key:
1. b) Grumpy
2. a) Frustrated
3. a) Happy

COMPARING FEELINGS

Answer Key:
1. b) She felt happy and warm.
2. a) Building a fort and playing with her mom.

FILL IN THE BLANKS

Answer Key:

1. grumpy
2. fort
3. warm
4. sunshine
5. feelings

VOCABULARY MATCH

Answer Key:
1. Grumpy – c) Feeling upset or annoyed.
2. Cozy – a) Warm and comfortable.
3. Fort – d) A fun hiding place made with blankets.
4. Sunshine – b) Bright light from the sun.
5. Feelings – e) Emotions like happy, sad, or excited.

9. Friendship Flowers

Story: Charlie Finds a Friend

Charlie was a shy little boy who loved playing with his toys.

But at school, he often played alone. During lunch, he sat by himself and watched other kids play on the swings and slide. He wished he had a friend but didn't know how to make one.

One day, Charlie saw a new girl, Lily, sitting alone under a tree. She looked sad. Charlie felt nervous, but he picked up his favorite toy car and walked over to her.

"Do you want to play?" Charlie asked, holding out his car.

Lily's face lit up. "Yes! I love cars!"

Charlie and Lily played together all afternoon. They laughed, took turns, and even made up a race game. Charlie felt happy—happier than he had felt in a long time.

From that day on, Charlie and Lily became best friends. They played together every day, shared their lunches, and helped each other in class.

Charlie learned that making friends wasn't so hard after all. All it took was kindness and a little courage.

Life Lesson:

Friends make life fun and meaningful! Charlie learned that friendship brings happiness. When we are kind and open to others, we can make wonderful friends who make our days brighter.

CHARACTER ANALYSIS

1) How did Charlie feel at the beginning of the story?
a) Happy
b) Shy and lonely
c) Excited

2) How did Charlie's feelings change by the end of the story?
a) He felt happy and made a friend.
b) He felt sad.
c) He felt angry.

3) What words describe Charlie? (Choose two)
a) Shy
b) Kind
c) Mean

MAKING PREDICTIONS

1) What do you think Charlie and Lily will do next?
a) Play more games together.
b) Stop being friends.
c) Go home.

2) Do you think they will meet new friends?
a) Yes
b) No

VOCABULARY MATCH

Match the word on the left with its correct meaning on the right.

Word	Meaning
1. Shy	a) Feeling good and joyful.
2. Kind	b) Feeling nervous around others.
3. Friend	c) Being brave to try something new.
4. Courage	d) Being nice and caring.
5. Happy	e) Someone you like and play with.

FILL IN THE BLANKS

Fill in the blanks with the correct word from the story:

Word Bank:
shy, happy, race, kindness, meaningful

1. Charlie was a _____ boy who loved playing with his toys.
2. Lily looked _____ when Charlie asked her to play.
3. Charlie and Lily played together and made up a _____ game.
4. Charlie learned that making friends takes _____ and courage.
5. Friends make life fun and _____.

ANSWERS

CHARACTER ANALYSIS

Answer Key:
1. b) Shy and lonely
2. a) He felt happy and made a friend.
3. a) Shy and b) Kind

MAKING PREDICTIONS

Answer Key:
1. a) Play more games together.
2. a) Yes

FILL IN THE BLANKS

Answer Key:

1. shy
2. happy
3. race
4. kindness
5. meaningful

VOCABULARY MATCH ACTIVITY

Answer Key:
1. Shy – b) Feeling nervous around others.
2. Kind – d) Being nice and caring.
3. Friend – e) Someone you like and play with.
4. Courage – c) Being brave to try something new.
5. Happy – a) Feeling good and joyful.

10. Conclusion: You Are a Star!

Look How Much You've Grown!

Wow! You've been on an incredible reading journey!

Along the way, you met amazing characters, explored new ideas, and learned important life lessons. Let's take a moment to celebrate everything you've discovered:

🌟 ***Kindness** – Sharing and helping others makes the world a better place.*
🌟 ***Honesty** – Telling the truth helps us build trust and feel proud of ourselves.*
🌟 ***Teamwork** – Working together makes big challenges easier to handle.*
🌟 ***Confidence** – Believing in yourself can help you try new things.*

🌟 **Patience** – Good things take time, and waiting can bring great rewards.

🌟 **Sharing** – Giving to others brings happiness to everyone.

🌟 **Caring for Nature** – Protecting our planet is an important job for all of us.

🌟 **Understanding Feelings** – It's okay to have different emotions, and we can express them in healthy ways.

🌟 **Friendship** – Friends make life fun and full of laughter!

Keep Reading, Keep Exploring! 📖✨

Stories are like magic keys that open doors to exciting adventures. Every time you read, you grow smarter, stronger, and more curious. So keep turning pages, asking questions, and discovering new worlds!

Activity: Your Turn to Shine! 🎨✏️

Think about everything you've learned in this book!
 🔹 What was your favorite story?
 🔹 Which life lesson meant the most to you?
 🔹 Did a story remind you of something in your own life?

Now, let's get creative!

✅ Draw a picture of your favorite moment in the book.
✅ Write a sentence about what you learned and why it's important to you.
✅ Share your drawing and thoughts with a friend, teacher, or family member!

You Are a Star! ⭐

Remember, you are AMAZING! Every story you read, every lesson you learn, and every new word you discover helps you shine even brighter. Keep reading, keep dreaming, and always believe in yourself—because you are a star!

We'd Love Your Feedback!

Please let us know how we're doing by leaving us a review.

APPENDIX -A : COMMON ACTION WORDS (VERBS) FOR FIRST GRADERS

Action Word	Example Sentence
Run	The boy can run fast.
Jump	The cat jumps high.
Laugh	Mia laughs with her friend.
Share	I share my toys with my brother.
Wait	We wait in line at the store.
Help	Sam helps his mom clean the table.
Think	I think before I speak.
Play	The kids play outside in the park.

APPENDIX -B : EMOTION WORDS AND HOW TO RECOGNIZE THEM

Emotion	How It Looks	Example Sentence
Happy 😊	Smiling, laughing, clapping	I feel happy when I play with my friends.
Sad 😢	Frowning, teary eyes, quiet	She felt sad when her balloon popped.
Angry 😡	Crossed arms, loud voice, red face	Tom was angry when he lost his toy.
Scared 😨	Wide eyes, shaking, hiding	The puppy was scared of the loud noise.
Excited 🎉	Jumping, big smiles, talking fast	I was excited for my birthday party.

APPENDIX -C : LIFE LESSONS FROM THE STORIES

Chapter	Story Title	Life Lesson
1	The Little Bird Who Shared	Sharing and helping others make everyone happy.
2	Lila and the Lost Marble	Honesty builds trust and makes us feel good.
3	The Ants and the Gigantic Apple	Teamwork helps us achieve amazing things.
4	Max Tries Something New	Believing in yourself leads to success.
5	The Caterpillar Who Waited	Good things take time and patience.
6	Mia and the Magic Crayons	Sharing brings joy to everyone.
7	Tommy and the Talking Tree	Taking care of the Earth is important.
8	Sasha's Cloudy Day	It's okay to have different emotions.

APPENDIX -D : EASY WORD ROOTS FOR KIDS

Word Root	Meaning	Example Words
Bio (Greek)	Life	Biology, Biography
Aqua (Latin)	Water	Aquarium, Aquatic
Tele (Greek)	Far	Telephone, Television
Auto (Greek)	Self	Autograph, Automobile
Port (Latin)	Carry	Transport, Portable
Vis (Latin)	See	Vision, Invisible
Graph (Greek)	Write	Photograph, Autograph
Terra (Latin)	Earth	Terrain, Territory
Ped (Latin)	Foot	Pedal, Pedestrian
Dent (Latin)	Tooth	Dentist, Dental

YOUNG WRITER SERIES - DR. FANATOMY

www.ingramcontent.com/pod-product-compliance
Lightning Source LLC
Chambersburg PA
CBHW082212070526
44585CB00020B/2376